Perfect
DEVON

JEN BRYANT

HALSGROVE

To Danny

First published in Great Britain in 2008

Copyright © Jen Bryant 2008

Title page image: *Criss-cross of hedges divide fields above the River Otter, near Monkton.*

British Library Cataloguing-in-Publication Data
A CIP record for this title is available from the British Library

ISBN 978 1 84114 714 7

HALSGROVE
Halsgrove House
Ryelands Industrial Estate
Bagley Road, Wellington,
Somerset TA21 9PZ
Tel: 01823 653777
Fax: 01823 216796
email: sales@halsgrove.com
website: www.halsgrove.com

Printed and bound by D'Auria Industrie Grafiche, Italy

INTRODUCTION

I have always lived in Devon. I was born in Braunton and brought up on a farm in Croyde, a small village on the North Devon coast. I don't think there is a better place to be a child. We had space, animals, nature, the beach, with everything revolving around the changing seasons. There was always something to see or do. This is where my love of Devon started and lasts to this day. When I married I only went as far as Okehampton for a short while after which we moved back to North Devon where we still live today.

After staying at home to bring up our two sons, I worked as a school secretary in a small village school in Abbotsham, a village just outside Bideford. After sixteen happy years I left and worked for a couple of years as a support assistant for people with special needs. During all of this time, we, as a family, walked, especially on Dartmoor. The better I got to know Dartmoor, the more I came to love it. I still feel pulled between the coast and the Moor.

I had always carried a compact 'point and shoot' camera when out walking but had more often than not been dissatisfied with the results. In 2000 I decided to do an evening class at a local school. I did one term learning how to use a camera, where the whole world of 'f' numbers and shutter speeds was revealed and at last, I was in control. The course also covered processing and printing black and white films. I loved every bit of it and carried on to do a second term following up with a course of printing classes. After you have the basics there is no better thing to do than take lots of pictures and that's just what I did. I now had two hobbies, walking and photography, pursuits made to go with each other.

I started to make and sell my own cards and now sell through my website (www.jenbryant.co.uk), various outlets including a stall in Tavistock Market and local agricultural shows.

I still use film and intend to for as long as I can. I am quite happy with the results and do not need the immediacy of digital capture. I find it exciting to wait for slides to come back from the lab to see what I've got. I carry two Nikon F80 bodies; one loaded with B&W film, the other with the wonderful Velvia slide film. I use 28-80 mm, 70-300 mm and 18-35 mm lenses and I always use a tripod. That makes my load quite a lot heavier than when I used to use a small compact camera. I think that the best times to be out are the hours before and after dawn and sunset. Dawn is the best time, most people are still in bed. The light can be incredible. The hour before sunset, with its intense light, is wonderful. At sunset I have noticed that most people leave as soon as the sun has set; if only they had stayed. The colour can stay in the sky for up to 40 minutes after the sun has gone and can become more and more intense and then suddenly fade. I consider it a privilege to experience these, sometime fleeting, moments.

When I was asked by Halsgrove to provide images for a book on Devon I was firstly thrilled quickly followed by panic. I have built up a reasonable stock of images of North Devon and Dartmoor, but for one reason or another, mainly to do with distance, I had little or nothing on South or East Devon. I bought maps and started planning immediately. It really has made me appreciate, even more than I did before, what a diverse and beautiful county Devon is. From North Devon, with its magnificent coastline, high rugged cliffs and long stretches of sandy surf beaches, to inland areas of gently undulating green farmland. Also included in North Devon is a small part of Exmoor with its heather covered rounded hills and deep coombes.

We then have Dartmoor, the last wilderness in the South of England, a wild barren place with its granite tors and prehistoric sites. Most of the great rivers of Devon rise here.

South Devon has a beautiful coastline with fine views at every point. The great estuaries of the Dart, the Erme and the Yealm with their beautiful hidden creeks, not forgetting the Avon and the Teign. It has beautiful rolling green hills with vibrant towns such as Modbury and Totnes with their diverse mixture of shops.

East Devon has a spectacular coast line, its 'Jurassic Coast', now internationally recognised. The red sandstone cliffs at Sidmouth are spectacular, and the creamy-white chalk cliffs with the sun on them at Beer Head are stunning. There are pretty villages scattered about in the valleys, Branscombe, Otterton and East Budleigh to name a few. Further north takes us to the edge of the Blackdown Hills, yet another area of outstanding beauty.

Devon then has its two cities of Plymouth and Exeter both overflowing with history and its towns from Tavistock to Barnstaple to Tiverton to genteel Sidmouth, all with their own unique identities.

I have thoroughly enjoyed my journey around my home county and have been constantly reminded of how lucky I am to live in Perfect Devon. I hope you enjoy it too.

Jen Bryant, 2008

A Ten Tors group sets off on a practice walk along the Devonport Leat
below Beardown Tor. Longaford Tor can be seen in the distance.

Becky Falls, on the Becka Brook near Manaton.

Tor's End, Belstone, in the golden light of dawn.

Looking from Belstone Ridge towards Steeperton Tor on one of those perfect winter days.

Bennett's Cross just before
the storm, one of the many it will
have weathered in its time.

Brentor Church lit by late evening sunlight.

Opposite: Black-a-tor Copse, an ancient dwarf oak wood on the West Okement River below Black Tor.

Thatched granite cottages at Buckland in the Moor.

A stunted hawthorn on the western slopes of Cox Tor glows red from the reflection of the setting sun.

Granite boulders worn smooth by the action of the water of the East Dart at Dartmeet.

Opposite: Looking down the Dart Valley from Sharp Tor just before sunrise.

Still waters – Fernworthy Reservoir.

Winter trees along the wall of Four Winds car park on Dartmoor, on the road between Merrivale and Rundlestone. This used to be a school for the quarry workers' children.

Fields of bluebells at Holwell Lawn, with Holwell Tor and Haytor in the background.

Opposite: The fantastic granite formations of Great Staple Tor silhouetted by the sunset.

The Cleave Inn – Lustleigh.

Mirror image – a still Spring evening at Meldon Reservoir.

Stormy skies at dawn on Dartmoor. Looking across Merrivale Stone Row towards Great Mis Tor.

Moretonhampstead on the north-eastern edge of Dartmoor.

Ponies in the pound at Merrivale on Dartmoor after being rounded up in the annual Pony Drift.

Opposite: The woods above Okehampton are full of bluebells during May.

The waters of the River Teign cascade over boulders as it leaves Dartmoor at Scorhill.

Mares' tails stream across the sky over the fissured granite of Saddle Tor.

Sheep eating their way over Belstone Ridge on Dartmoor.

Sheepstor Church sits in a wide landscape of tors and trees.

A touch of frost at dawn over Taw Marsh on Dartmoor. Steeperton crowned with its hut is in the distance.

A majestic archway of beech trees near Bridestowe.

Drifting snow and windblown hawthorn on Belstone Ridge.

Warm evening light and long shadows over fields in West Devon.

Wistman's Wood – an ancient place where the devil is supposed to ride out at
dusk with his wisht hounds in order to hunt for lost souls.

Opposite: Widgery Cross stands pround on Brat Tor. It celebrate Queen Victoria's Golden Jubilee.

The tidal road at Aveton Gifford on the River Avon begins to appear as the tide recedes.

Moonrise over the sand dunes at Bantham.

The setting sun catches the light in the lighthouse on Berry Head.

A calm September day
at Brixham Harbour.

Incredible sunset behind Burgh Island.

Part of Canonteign Falls
near Chudleigh. This is the
highest waterfall in England.

41

The rainbow before the rain at Cockwood, between Starcross and Dawlish.

Ermington sits in the shelter of a hill, with Dartmoor rising up behind.

Frogmore Creek, off the Kingsbridge Estuary, in the winter sun.

The dramatic cliffs between Hallsands and Start Point. The ruins
of Old Hallsands sits at the bottom of the cliffs.

Hope's Nose, where gold was found in the past but was too expensive to mine.

Looking down the estuary from Kingsbridge before dawn.

Boats moored up in the Kingsbridge Estuary seen from East Portlemouth.

Nature manages not to clash in the gardens at Lukesland near Ivybridge.

Powderham Castle near Starcross, historic home to the Earls of Devon, is over 600 years old.

Opposite: A peaceful morning on the Yealm Estuary at Newton Ferrers.

The narrow mouth of the Dart Estuary was protected by two
fortified castles, Dartmouth Castle and Kingswear Castle.

A train passes walkers on the sea wall between Dawlish and Teignmouth.

The Ness at Shaldon stands overlooking the mouth of the Teign.

Incoming tide at Slapton Sands.

Ducks on the stream at South Pool near Kingsbridge.

Boats drawn up on the shore in The Salty, Teignmouth.

Looking towards Thatcher Rock from Meadfoot beach.

Opposite: Winter sunrise – Teignmouth Pier.

The Thurlestone, a natural stone archway fashioned by the sea.

The tide flows over the shingle at Torcross.

In Ness Cove beneath The Ness at Shaldon.

Opposite: Looking from above Labrador Bay towards The Ness and across the bay to Exmouth.

Wild garlic in woods at Yealmpton.

The bridge over the Dart at Totnes, located here in historic times at the highest point navigable on the Dart and the lowest place at which a bridge could be built.

Buildings seem to be stacked up as they climb the hill above the river at Dartmouth.

The town of Dartmouth is dominated by Britannia Royal Naval College.

The new Taw Bridge opened in 2007 which, although controversial, has helped
traffic run smoothly through Barnstaple after years of congestion.

Butchers' Row in Barnstaple was built in Victorian times. All the shops were once
butchers but now other, mainly food, outlets are included.

Legend has it that Tom Faggus, a well known Exmoor highwayman, was trapped on
Barnstaple Long Bridge from either end by pursuers. He encouraged his horse
to jump the parapet of the bridge and they both swam to safety.

Queen Anne presides over
Queen Anne's Walk in Barnstaple.
Here merchants used to barter and strike
a deal over the Tome Stone which is
in the archway below the statue.

71

Feeding the swans at Exeter Quay.

Mol's Coffee House in Cathedral Close, Exeter. The front was supposed to be like the prow of a galleon. Both Drake and Raleigh were regulars here.

Exeter Cathedral, built of warm-coloured Beer Stone.
There has been a cathedral on this spot since 1050AD.

Sir Francis Drake looks out over the Sound from his plinth on Plymouth Hoe.

Smeaton's Tower guarded The Eddystone Rocks until the 1870s when it was found that the rocks it stood on were being eroded. The lighthouse was later dismantled and rebuilt on Plymouth Hoe.

Reflections of Sidmouth.

The striking new bridge in Torquay Harbour links the north and south pier and enables people to walk all lthe way round the inner harbour for the first time.

Torquay's Pavilion stands next to colourful gardens on the front.

Torquay sunset.

The Princess Pier in Torquay started life as a groyne but was embellished
with wrought iron and decking and became a pier in 1894.

Pastoral scene near Aylesbeare.

Fishing boats and equipment on the beach at Beer.

Cottages next to Bickleigh Castle on a bright, frosty morning.

Opposite: Looking east from Beer towards Seaton showing the beautiful chalk cliffs.

View over lush green fields on the edge of the Blackdown Hills.

Thatched cottages, complete with doves, play their part in making
Branscombe a very attractive and peaceful village.

Budlake Post Office on the Killerton Estate.
It is kept in the style of a 1950s post office.

Long shadows across the pebble ridge above the beach at Budleigh Salterton.

Beautiful frosty morning – the Valley of the Burn, a small tributary of the Exe, near Bickleigh.

Oilseed rape and blue skies near Crediton.

Pre-dawn in the Culm Valley area.

Opposite: Beech leaves and bluebells in Dunsford Wood near Steps Bridge.

Exmouth beach from Orcombe Point with Dawlish Warren
on the opposite side of the Exe Estuary.

Golden light just before the sun disappears at Exmouth.

Calm evening on the
Grand Western Canal near Tiverton.

The lovely green valley which leads from Branscombe down to the sea.

Opposite: The Geoneedle at Orcombe Point above Exmouth. This marks the most westerly point of the Jurassic Coast.

A still evening at Ottermouth, Budleigh Salterton.

The ridges of a newly-planted field of potatoes near Tiverton disappear into the mist.

Sampford Peverell Church reflected in the Great Western Canal on a beautiful still day.

Incoming tide at Seaton, with the white chalk cliffs at Beer Head in the distance.

The incredible red Devonian
Sandstone cliffs looking
back towards Sidmouth.

103

A walk along Jacob's Ladder beach as the tide goes out.

The breeze rustles through a wheat field near Thorverton.

Evening light highlights the strata in the cliffs at Abbotsham.

Still reflections at Appledore as the clouds take on a pink tinge just before sunrise.

A line of beech trees march up the hill on the edge of Brendon Common on Exmoor.

A swan glides on the Torridge upstream from the graceful old Bideford Bridge.

Charles Kingsley awaits sunrise on the Pill at Bideford.

Blackchurch Rock at Mouth Mill,
Hartland, where the whole coastline
has a dramatic wild geological make-up.

Ducks on one of the dykes on Braunton Marsh.

Opposite: Sunset at the beach at Blackpool Mill, Hartland.

Poppies flower in the area covered by Braunton Great Field.

Cottage at Bucks Mills, a small village strung out along a steep valley down to the sea.

The jagged coastline on the North coast with Bull Point lighthouse in the distance.

Cottages on the square at Chittlehampton.

The harbour wall at Clovelly, deserted on an early summer morning.

The unique cobbled
village of Clovelly tumbles
down a steep hill to the sea.

A pretty back street in Combe Martin.

MARINE
COTTAGE

The sun breaks through the clouds on the gently rolling green Devon countryside near Chittlehampton.

Early sun touches the buildings at Croyde Bay with its old lime kiln.

Beautiful snowy day on Exmoor.

Rosebay willowherb makes a striking display along the North coast towards Foreland Point.

Ash Mill, a typical small North Devon hamlet.

Masses of thrift cover the cliffs at Hartland.

Opposite: Hartland Lighthouse looking out towards Lundy Island.

A hazy sunrise over Appledore.

Looking down on Ilfracombe Harbour from Beacon Point as it is bathed in early morning light.

A boat awaits the tide;
a peaceful evening at Instow.

Lifeguards watch over swimmers on the wide expanse of Westward Ho! Beach.

Town Lane on the edge of Little Torrington makes for a pretty walk in Spring.

Fields of gold – acres of oilseed rape near Merton in North Devon.

The jagged slate rocks of Morte Point, the site of many shipwrecks. The very name is said by some to be taken from the French for death. Because of the often rough conditions in the area, Morte Point is referred to by some as 'the place God made last and the devil will take first'.

Sand dunes almost as far as the eye can see. Braunton Burrows is the largest sand dune system in the UK and has been designated a UNESCO Biosphere Reserve.

Sea mist holds a veil over the sea at the foot of Hangman, the highest sea cliff in England.

Enjoying a cream tea at Stoke, Hartland, on a perfect summer's day.

A ewe and her lambs enjoy the warmth from the first rays of sun on a winter day.

North Road. This stretch of the coastal path between Lynton and Lee Bay
clings to the side of the cliff and is not for the faint hearted.

A lone winter tree in twilight, the time known in Devon as 'dimpsey' when the sun has set and before night sets in.

This must be one of the most picturesque cricket grounds in the country, set in the Valley of Rocks near Lynton.

The waterfall on Hoar Oak Water just before it meets the East Lyn at Watersmeet on Exmoor.

Opposite: Castle Rock at the western end of the Valley of Rocks rises vertically from the sea.

Silhouetted trees at dusk near Jacobstowe.